LOST AT SEA

Frances Ridley

Copyright © ticktock Entertainment Ltd 2008

First published in Great Britain in 2008 by ticktock Media Ltd,
2 Orchard Business Centre, North Farm Road, Tunbridge Wells, Kent, TN2 3XF

ticktock project editor: Ruth Owen
ticktock project designer: Sara Greasley
ticktock picture researcher: Lizzie Knowles

With thanks to series editors Honor Head and Jean Coppendale

Thank you to Lorraine Petersen and the members of nasen

ISBN 978 1 84696 709 2 pbk

Printed in China

Picture credits (t=top; b=bottom; c=centre; l=left; r=right):
AP/ PA Photos: 21c. Julian Baum: 18-19, 28b. Tobias Bernhard/ zefa/ Corbis: 10t. Tobias Bernhard/ Getty Images: 26-27. Bruce Brown/ Superstock: 1, 14. Brandon Cole/ www.brandoncole.com: 22. Tim Cuff/ Alamy: 13, 28t. epa/ Corbis: 5 inset. Getty Images: 15. iStock: 2. David Lyons/ Alamy: 12t. Newspix/ Steve Brennan: 23. David Osborn/ Alamy: 11t. Pink Lady Atlantic First via Getty Images: 6c. Reuters/ Ho: 21t, 21b. Reuters/ Pool: 11b. Macro Secchi/ Alamy: 17. Shutterstock: OFC, 4-5, 7, 8-9, 20-21 background, 28-29 background, 31. Sipa Press/ Rex Features: 24-25. Superstock Inc/ Superstock: 29.

Every effort has been made to trace copyright holders, and we apologise in advance for any omissions. We would be pleased to insert the appropriate acknowledgments in any subsequent edition of this publication.

Contents

CHAPTER 1

KILLER SEAS

A shipwreck is a warning. Beware of the sea!

Modern steel ships are safer than old wooden ships. But shipwrecks still happen.

In 2002, an oil tanker called *Prestige* got into trouble off the coast of Spain. It suffered damage during a very bad storm.

The tanker broke in half and sank. The crew were rescued. But 70,000 tonnes of oil spilled into the sea. This caused terrible damage to beaches and wildlife in the area.

The sea can be a killer.

What does it take to survive?

CHAPTER 2

FIGHTING THE SEA

On 30 June, 2004, four rowers set off to break a record.

The four men wanted to row the Atlantic Ocean from west to east in under 55 days.

Atlantic Ocean

The route was 3,380 kilometres long.

The rowers were Peter Bray, Jonathan Gornall, John Wills and the skipper, Mark Stubbs. Their boat was called *Pink Lady*.

The route was filled with danger.

There were four times as many icebergs as normal and terrible storms.

On 6 August, the team were told they were sailing into the tail-end of Hurricane Alex!

Some icebergs are as big as mountains.

There was nothing the rowers could do.
They put on their survival jackets and waited.

Then, in the middle of the night, disaster struck!

"The wave sounded like an express train. It hit the boat like a missile in the dark."
Jonathan Gornall

A freak wave, over 18 metres high, crashed down onto *Pink Lady*. The wave turned the boat upside-down and smashed it in two.

**The crew climbed into the life raft.
They sent out a distress signal.**

They were tossed about on huge, icy waves for seven hours.

Life raft

MAP OF RECORD-BREAKING ROW

The rowers set off from Newfoundland, in Canada, on 30 June, 2004.

Atlantic Ocean

650 kilometres

Map scale

An RAF Nimrod plane found them. It sent out a Mayday signal.

Several hours later a container ship rescued them.

Their boat was cut in half by a storm. They were 480 kilometres west of the Scilly Isles.

Falmouth, UK

Scilly Isles

CHAPTER 3

RACING DISASTER!

In August 1979, disaster struck the Fastnet Yacht Race.

Fastnet Lighthouse

The yachts sail from Cowes on the Isle of Wight to the Fastnet Lighthouse. They sail around the lighthouse and back to Plymouth.

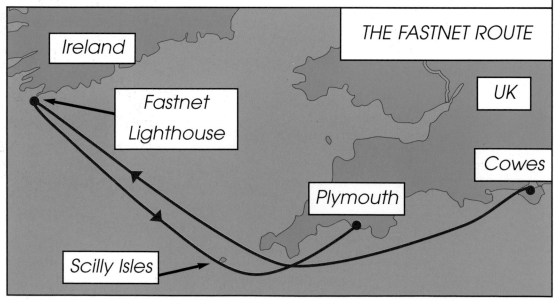

THE FASTNET ROUTE

Ireland

Fastnet Lighthouse

UK

Cowes

Plymouth

Scilly Isles

The 303 yachts set off in the morning in good weather. But within eight hours, everything had changed!

The yachts sailed into a freak storm.

Matthew Sheahan was 17. He was with his father, David Sheahan. They were on their yacht, called *Grimalkin*. All day the storm battered *Grimalkin*.

That night it got worse.

Reconstruction

Safety harness

The boat rolled from side to side. The crew were flung into the waves again and again.
Their safety harnesses pulled them back.

Then a huge wave hit the boat.
David Sheahan was knocked unconscious.
The boat turned upside-down.

When it flipped back, Matthew saw a body in the sea.

He was sure it was his father.

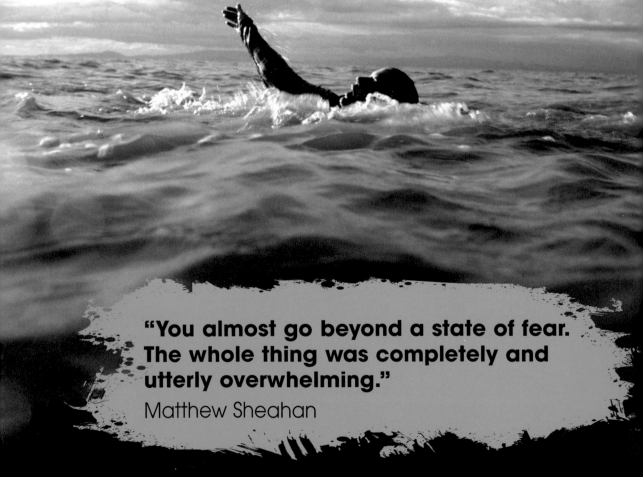

"You almost go beyond a state of fear. The whole thing was completely and utterly overwhelming."
Matthew Sheahan

The *Grimalkin* was badly damaged.
Matthew and the crew scrambled into the life raft.

Hours later they were picked up by a rescue helicopter.

They were the lucky ones.
They had survived.

Winchman

A winchman from a rescue helicopter is lowered onto Grimalkin.

Fifteen of the racers died.
David Sheahan's body was never found.

CHAPTER 4

UNDERWATER HORROR

On 4 August, 2005, the Russian mini-sub *Priz* became tangled up in fishing nets.

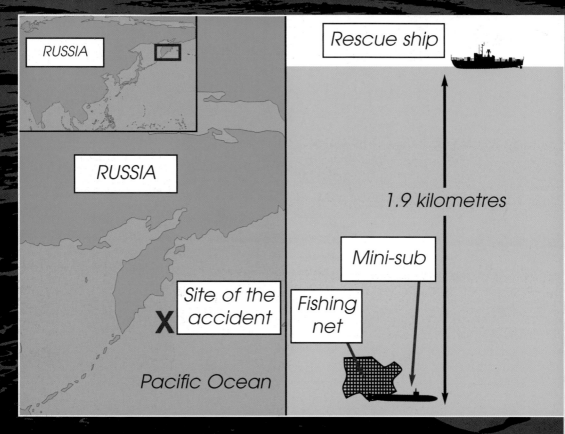

The mini-sub was too deep for its crew to escape.

The Russian Navy looped a cable around the mini-sub to pull it up. But it wouldn't budge.

The mini-sub's crew turned off power to save electricity. They kept still and breathed lightly to save oxygen.

The men put on thermal suits to keep warm.

They were hungry and thirsty. The sub did not have enough supplies, only a little water and some biscuits.

Scorpio 45

Britain sent a rescue team and an underwater robot rescue sub, called *Scorpio 45*.

The robot is controlled from the surface. It can go to places too dangerous or too deep for human divers.

Scorpio 45 was lowered down on a cable. It began to cut through the nets.

It took several hours, but finally, the mini-sub was cut free. *Scorpio 45* was just in time.

The Russian crew had been trapped underwater for 76 hours.

They had one hour of oxygen left!

CHAPTER 5

AGAINST THE ODDS

Story 1 – swept out to sea

On 26 December, 2004, there was an earthquake under the Indian Ocean. It caused a huge wave called a tsunami.

The wave was 9 metres high. It smashed into the coastline of many countries in Asia. The tsunami disaster killed 200,000 people.

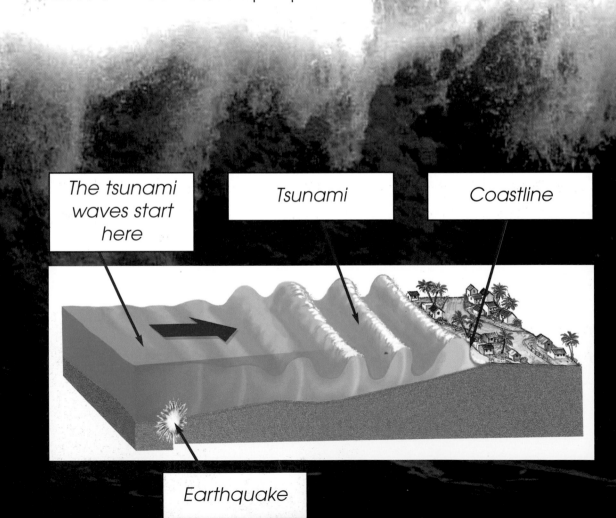

The tsunami waves start here

Tsunami

Coastline

Earthquake

Ari Afrizal was swept out to sea by the huge wave.

First he clung to a plank of wood, then a leaking fishing boat. He ate coconuts that floated by. He saw many dead bodies in the water.

Raft with hut

One day, a huge raft floated by. Ari managed to climb on board. The raft had a hut on it and a large bottle of water.

After 15 days at sea, Ari was finally rescued by a container ship.

Raft

Ship

Story 2 – swimming with sharks

In 2004, three Australian children took a boat trip with their parents and baby brother.

The boat's engine failed and the boat capsized.

Tiger sharks sometimes attack humans.

There were tiger sharks in the water. The sea was rough.

The parents told the older children to swim to some rocks. The parents and baby brother stayed in the water where the boat had capsized.

The children swam 9 kilometres to the rocks. They spent three days on the rocks. But there was no food or water.

Matu Island

1.6 km

Rocks

So, the children swam another 1.6 kilometres from the rocks to the island of Matu. No one lives on Matu, but the children found some food – coconuts and shellfish.

After six days they were rescued by their uncle in his boat. Their parents and baby brother were never found.

Story 3 – lost in a freezing ocean

In 1997, Tony Bullimore's yacht capsized during a round-the-world race.

Tony was in the Southern Ocean. He was about 800 kilometres from Antarctica. The water here is so cold, it can kill a person in minutes. Thankfully, Tony had put on his thermal survival suit.

Antarctica

Southern Ocean

Yacht

Rescuers

EXIDE CHALLENGER

"I thought it would never happen."
Tony Bullimore, when he was rescued

Tony made a place to sit in the upside-down cabin. He put his emergency rations and fresh water there, too. He was wet and freezing cold.

It took five days for rescuers to find the yacht. They were sure Tony could not have survived. The rescuers banged on the yacht's hull. They were amazed to hear Tony bang back!

Tony had run out of fresh water. He had no feeling left in his hands and feet. He was exhausted...

...but he was alive!

Hull

Tony

33

CHAPTER 6 SURVIVORS

During World War 2, a man named Poon Lim was a sailor on a British ship. His ship was taking supplies to the war zones.

The ship was hit by a German torpedo in the Atlantic Ocean.

Poon found a life raft. He lived on the raft for 133 days.

He stayed alive by catching seabirds and fish. He ate them raw and drank their blood instead of water.

What does it take to survive?

Strength

The three Australian children swam over 10 kilometres.

The crew of the *Grimalkin* battled the storm for a day and a night.

Skills

The crews of the *Grimalkin* and the *Pink Lady* were expert sailors.

A cool head

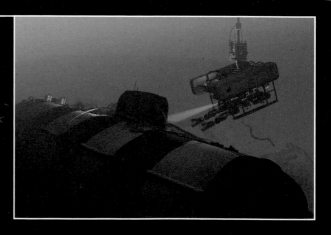

The Russians trapped in the mini-sub didn't panic. They breathed lightly to save oxygen.

A strong stomach!

In 1816, a French ship, called the *Medusa*, became trapped on a sandbank. Some people tried to escape from the sinking ship on a raft. Others stayed with the wreck.

There was no food and very little fresh water. People began to die.

After many weeks, the survivors were so hungry they ate the bodies of their dead shipmates.

Could you?

NEED TO KNOW WORDS

capsize When a boat turns upside-down in the water.

container ship A ship that carries goods using containers – large, metal, room-sized boxes.

crew The men and women who sail or row a boat.

emergency rations Packets of high-energy food. This food helps people to survive until they are rescued.

hull The bottom, sides and deck of a ship.

hypothermia When a person's body temperature gets so low it causes damage to their body and brain. It can cause death.

life raft An inflatable lifeboat.

Mayday signal A call for help using a radio signal. It is used by ships and planes.

mini-sub A small submarine. Mini-subs are often used for rescues. They can be manned or unmanned.

route The course you take to get somewhere.

safety harness A harness that attaches a sailor to the yacht.

Scorpio 45 A robot rescue sub with cameras and cutting equipment. It can pass supplies, such as food and oxygen, to a trapped submarine. It uses the submarine's escape hatch to pass the supplies.

skipper The captain of a ship.

survival jacket (or life jacket) A sleeveless jacket that is filled with air or made of foam. It helps you to float in the water. Survival jackets are often bright colours. This helps rescuers spot them easily.

thermal suit An all-over waterproof survival suit. It keeps heat in and the cold out.

torpedo A missile that is fired underwater.

Yacht A sailing boat used for cruising or racing.

SURVIVAL FACTS

- You can survive without food for about a month.

- You will survive for less than a week without water.

- You must protect yourself from hot sun. You need to make a shelter, or keep your head, face, shoulders and arms covered.

- In cold and icy seas, hypothermia is a danger. Keep your head wrapped up to stop heat loss. Stay still to save energy.

- Sea water is too salty to drink. It will damage your blood cells and your kidneys. It is better to drink the blood of fish or birds.

GET ONLINE!

Websites
http://news.bbc.co.uk/onthisday/hi/witness/august/14/newsid_3541000/3541260.stm
Listen to Matthew Sheahan's audio account of his experience

http://news.bbc.co.uk/1/hi/uk/4128716.stm
Watch videos about the rescue of the Russian mini-sub

http://news.bbc.co.uk/2/hi/uk_news/3547532.stm
See pictures of *The Pink Lady's* record attempt

INDEX